London
A Time Traveller's Guide

MOIRA BUTTERFIELD

W
FRANKLIN WATTS
LONDON • SYDNEY

This edition published 2014
by Franklin Watts
338 Euston Road, London NW1 3BH

Franklin Watts Australia
Level 17/207 Kent Street, Sydney,
NSW 2000

A CIP catalogue record for this book
is available from the British Library

Dewey Classification: 914

ISBN: 978 1 4451 2924 2

Printed in China

Editor-in-Chief: John C. Miles
Editor: Sarah Ridley
Art direction: Peter Scoulding
Designer: Stephen Prosser
Artwork: John Alston
Picture researcher: Diana Morris

Franklin Watts is a division of
Hachette Children's Books,
an Hachette UK company.

www.hachette.co.uk

Note to Teachers and Parents:
Every effort has been made to
ensure that the websites listed in this
book are suitable for children, that
they are of the highest educational
value, and that they contain no
inappropriate or offensive material.
However, because of the nature
of the internet, it is impossible to
guarantee that the content of these
sites will not be altered. We strongly
recommend that internet access is
supervised by a responsible adult.

Picture credits:
Mira Agron/Dreamstime: 43b.
Andresr/Shutterstock: front cover br.
Art Archive/Alamy: 9t, 22b.
Art Directors & Trip/Alamy: 22tr.
The Art Gallery Collection/Alamy: 33c.
Anthony Baggett/Dreamstime: 29b.
Bambuh/Shutterstock: 27t.
Sergey Belov/istockphoto: 55cr.
Bibliothèque Nationale/Wikipedia: 23tc.
Bloomberg/Getty Images: 56br.
boumen&japet/Shutterstock: 13tc.
British Library/Wikipedia: 16bl, 21tr.
Cervus35/Flickr: 13cl.
Christapper/Shutterstock: 54bc.
Christies Images/Superstock: 23b, 32c.
Chunni4691/Shutterstock: 47b.
Robert Churchill/istockphoto: 54c.
Corbis: front cover cb, 48c, 48b, 49t.
Daily Herald Archive/Getty Images: 51t.
Claudio Divizia/istockphoto: front cover tr.
Dorling Kindersley/istockphoto: 12b.
Chris Dorney/Dreamstime: 33b.
Michael Dwyer/Alamy: 28cl, 28cr.
Mark Eaton/Dreamstime: 35b.
Mary Evans Picture Library: 38br.
David Garry/istockphoto: 19c.
Jeff Gilbert/Alamy: 21br.
Godrick/Dreamstime: 31b.
© Robert Graves/Didier Madoc-Jones:
59tl, 59tr.
Chris Harvey/Shutterstock: 55b.
Rubén Hidalgo/istockphoto: 7tc, 11c.
The Hoberman Collection/Alamy: 24b.
Neil Holmes/Alamy: 34c.
Angelo Hornak/Alamy: 17c.
Robert Howlett/Wikipedia: front cover cl.
David Hughes/Shutterstock: 27b inset.
Hulton Archive/Getty Images: 50b.
Hulton Deutsch/Corbis: 53tr.
Dragos Daniel Iliescu/Dreamstime: 54br.
Interfoto/Alamy: 52b.
Janne1/Dreamstime: 32cl.
Sylvie Jarrossay/Alamy: 39b.
Pete Jennings/www.ealdfaeder.org: 6bc,
6br, 14cl, 14c, 15cl.
Denis Jones/Associated Newspapers/Rex
Features: 57t.
Keystone/Getty Images: 51c.
Kimragaya/Dreamstime: 43c.
Georgios Kollidas/istockphoto: 38bl.
Vladimir Korostyshevskiy /Shutterstock: 11t.
Jan Kranedonk/Dreamstime: 42b.
Kuttelvaserova/Shutterstock: 22tc.
The Lady's Magazine And Museum: 38c.
London Fire Brigade/Mary Evans PL: 31t.
Lordprice Collection/Alamy: 37c.
David Mantel/istockphoto: 55t.
Metropolitan Railway 1924: 46c.
meunierd/Shutterstock: 10b.
Douglas Miller/Hulton Archive/Getty
Images: 50c.
© MOL: 13tr, 13bc, 17b, 18b, 30cr, 37b.
© MOLAS: 11b, 13br.
Christine Mowlam/Franklin Watts: 16t.
NASA/GSFC/MITI/ERSDAC/JAROS, and U.S./
Japan ASTER Science Team: 7b.
Nancy Nehring/istockphoto: 55cl.

Hein Nouwens/Shutterstock: 10c.
nrg123/Shutterstock: 6tl.
ODA: 9b.
Only Fabrizio/Shutterstock: 13cr.
oversnap/istockphoto: 49b.
Pen_85/Shutterstock: 35t.
Roger Philpott/The Costume Store www.
thecostumestoreonline.co.uk : 24cl, 24cr,
27cl.
Peter Phipp/Trailshots/Alamy: 18c.
Photogènes: 7trb, 11cb, 15bl, 23b, 25c,
30cl, 41b, 45b, 47tl.
Pictorial Press/Alamy: 45c.
Popperfoto/Getty Images: 51b.
Portsmouth Historic Dockyard: 33t.
The Print Collector /Alamy: 42c.
Prisma Archivo/Alamy: 20c.
Miki R/ Shutterstock: front cover main bg,
back cover main bg.
Geoffrey Robinson/Rex Features: 58cl.
Rolls Press/Popperfoto/Getty Images: 53tl.
Valentina_S/Shutterstock: 15t.
Steve Sant/Alamy: 19t.
Thorsten Schmitt/Shutterstock: 59c.
Science & Society PL/Superstock: 40b, 42t,
46b.
Jeremy Selwyn/Evening Standard/Rex
Features: 56bl.
sgame/Shutterstock: front cover bgc, back
cover c.
Mick Sharp/LoopmImages/Alamy: 15cr.
Dmitriy Shironosov/Shutterstock: 59bc.
Shutterstock: 25b, 52br.
sky earth/Shutterstock: 58t.
Sponner/Shutterstock: 27c.
Laszio Szirtesi/Shutterstock: 26t.
Ray Tang/Rex Features: 53b, 57bl.
Amoret Tanner Collection/Art Archive:
44b.
tele52/Shutterstock: 7bc.
3D stock/Shutterstock: 58cr.
Jason Timson/Rex Features: 57br.
Trinity Mirror/Mirrorpix/Alamy: 52cl.
20th Century Fox: 58b.
Renee Vititoe/Shutterstock: front cover c.
Duncan Walker/istockphoto: 39t, 43b.
L Watcharapol/Shutterstock: 7tr, 23tr,
37cb.
Watts: front cover bl, 26b, 29c, 44cl, 44cr.
Christine Webb/Alamy: 21t.
Margaret Bourke White/Time Life/Getty
Images: 47tr.
widewallpapers.net: 59br.
Wikipedia: 16cl, 16br, 17t, 30b, 31c, 32b,
36t.
Chris Williams/istockphoto: 19b.
Rob Wilson/Dreamstime: 39c.
woodsy/Shutterstock: front cover tl.
Padma Yogini/Shutterstock: 27b.

Every attempt has been made to
clear copyright. Should there be any
inadvertent omission, please apply to
the publisher for rectification.

Contents

Enter the time machine

London is thousands of years old, so when you walk its busy streets you are standing on top of history. Relics of the past – ancient treasures and long-forgotten buildings – lie hidden beneath the crowds and the brand new tower blocks of today. Imagine you could step into a time machine (it's waiting for you on the right) and take a tour through London centuries ago, to discover some of those hidden secrets. Fasten your time-travelling seatbelt and get ready for the ride!

Time Traveller's Instructions

Here's what you will find as you make your journey.

Maps of London
All travellers need maps, even time travellers. Study them to find out what London was like, and where to look for historical clues today.

People
On your trip, we'll introduce you to some Londoners from long ago. They will usually be children, and they won't mind showing you around.

Clothes
If you want to time travel through London without looking very strange, you'll need to wear the clothes that Londoners wore in the past. Ideas for these are provided along the journey.

Timelines
Sometimes London's history gets complicated, so occasionally there are mini timelines to help you understand what's been going on.

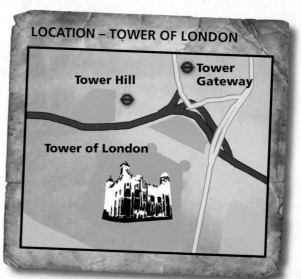

LOCATION – TOWER OF LONDON

Tower Hill

Tower Gateway

Tower of London

'Hello! Come and meet us on page 14.'

- First hunters arrived in the area about 750,000 years ago.

6

Avoid danger!

You'll need to watch out when you travel into the past! London has occasionally been a very dangerous place. At different times during its history there have been fearsome attacks by warrior armies, terrible plagues, fires raging and deadly bombs falling.

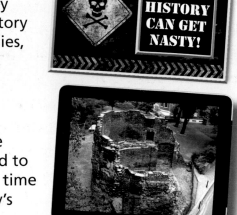

DANGER! HISTORY CAN GET NASTY!

Back to the 21st century

Your time travel will help you to spot some of the parts of London's history that have survived to modern times. After each time-travelling trip the time machine will bring you back to see some of today's sights that are connected to the city's past.

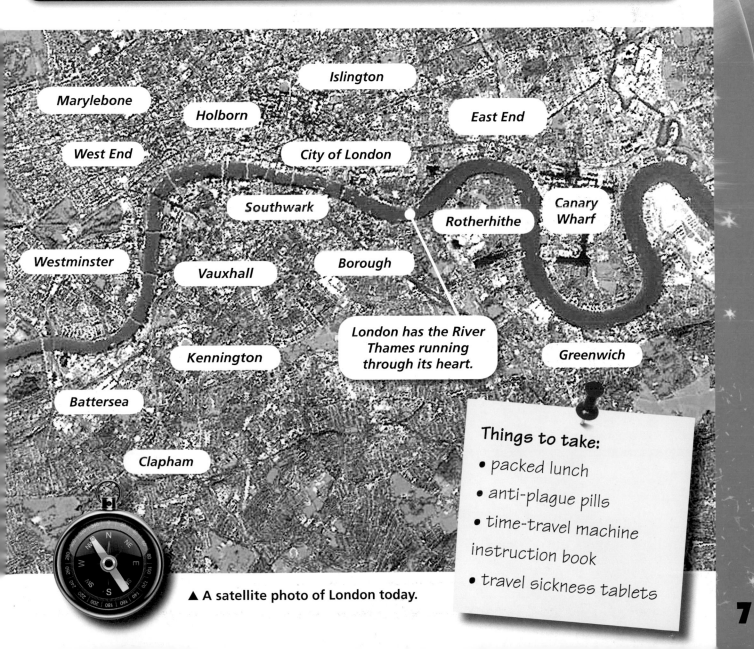

Islington

Marylebone

Holborn

East End

West End

City of London

Southwark

Canary Wharf

Rotherhithe

Westminster

Borough

Vauxhall

London has the River Thames running through its heart.

Kennington

Greenwich

Battersea

Clapham

Things to take:
- packed lunch
- anti-plague pills
- time-travel machine instruction book
- travel sickness tablets

▲ A satellite photo of London today.

Witness a mystery

The time machine has brought you to where London will be found one day, but there are no busy streets or buildings yet, just a boggy marsh. You'll recognise one thing though – the River Thames. On the riverbank there are a few round huts and a group of people. You are in the Iron Age, and you are about to witness a religious ceremony.

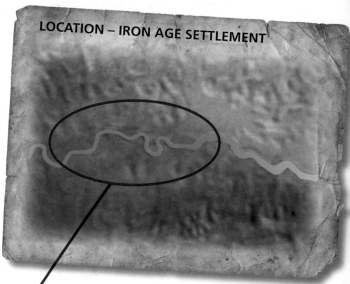

LOCATION – IRON AGE SETTLEMENT

London will grow up in this area.

◯ Your Destination

You need to know a bit more about where you have landed. The very first humans hunted in the London area about 750,000 years ago. Then people began to farm as well as hunt, and a few families settled near the river. They learnt how to make bronze, in a period of time now called the Bronze Age. Then they learnt how to make iron tools, in a time we call the Iron Age. Now they live in simple huts, grow a few crops and fish in the river.

✳ Lots of small streams run across the marshy countryside. People build their huts in places where they can easily cross the river.

✳ Wooden walkways are built over the boggiest areas. Remains of one have been found at Greenwich, dating to 6,000 years ago. That's about 3,000 years older than Stonehenge.

✳ Local people believe the river is a place where magic spirits live. They throw offerings into the water to please them.

Chelsea Bridge: Lots of river treasures, and an Iron Age carved head.

Westminster Underground Station: Very ancient hunting tools.

Stratford: Evidence of Bronze Age huts.

Under Waterloo Bridge: Iron Age horned helmet.

River near Battersea Bridge: Beautiful bronze shield and cauldron.

Greenwich: Ancient wooden walkway, skeletons and evidence of huts.

Woolwich: Remains of an Iron Age fort.

✳ Local tribes sometimes fight each other. Finds include a Bronze Age shield with a spear stuck through it.

✳ By the Iron Age, local tribes, such as the Trinovantes, live in the area. Each tribe has its own territory.

✳ Finds from early London are on display at the British Museum and the Museum of London. There is still much we don't know.

▲ This map shows some of the places where exciting ancient finds have been made.

◯ Time traveller's timeline - - - - - - - - - - - - - - - - - ➤

● The first hunters arrived in the area about 750,000 years ago.

● Bronze Age 2200–750BCE People settle and farm.

● Iron Age 750BCE–43CE People learn to make iron tools.

A magical shield

The people you can see standing by the river are carrying something shiny. It is a beautifully made shield of bronze and wood, decorated with swirling patterns and pieces of polished red glass. It is not being used for fighting, though. Instead, the leader of the tribe is throwing it in the river, during a religious ceremony.

✪ The shield is a very valuable treasure for the tribe. It has taken a lot of skill to make it, perhaps especially for this occasion.

✪ The tribe may have won a battle, or they want to win one soon against their neighbouring enemies. They are offering the shield to the river gods, to thank them or to ask for their help.

✪ In modern times, the shield is on display in the British Museum. It was found under Battersea Bridge, which crosses the Thames, but we don't know exactly when it was thrown in.

⊙ What to wear

Swap your clothes for an outfit that would have been worn in the Iron Age. Clothing was made of animal skins or rough cloth dyed with natural dyes.

Boys wore a tunic with a belt and a cloak pinned with a brooch.

Girls wore a long dyed woollen dress with a belt and a cloak, fastened by a brooch. Clothing fabric came in shades of brown, red, green or blue.

⊙ Back to the 21st century: Skeletons on the site

The 2012 Olympic site is one of London's newest attractions, but when redevelopment started, archaeologists found that early Londoners had settled there thousands of years ago. They found evidence of round huts built in the Bronze Age. The huts were circular, with a pole in the middle and a thatched roof on top.

Iron Age skeletons were found in graves buried in the area that eventually became the Olympic Aquatics Centre. A flint axe from 4,000 years ago turned up on the site. It seems that a prehistoric Londoner came hunting here, perhaps running and throwing spears long before the Olympic athletes!

▲ *Iron Age skeletons found on the site of the Olympic Park.*

Run for your life!

There's something wrong. Can you smell burning? And why are people running past in panic? They're trying to escape a screaming warrior-queen named Boudica, with red hair flowing down her back, waving a spear as she urges her chariot horses forward. Her blue-painted warriors don't look friendly, either. You are doomed if they see you, so stay inside the time machine and press the 'go' button quickly!

LOCATION – WALBROOK STREAM, NEAR THE BANK OF ENGLAND

Bank of England

Bank Station

The Mansion House

St Stephen Walbrook

What to wear

It isn't safe to leave your time machine today, but if you do, put on the clothes that someone might have worn in Roman London.

Girls wore a long tunic called a stolla, with a shawl called a palla and a brooch to hold it in place.

Boys wore a knee-length tunic and sometimes a cloak or a toga, along with sandals.

Your Destination

In 43CE southern Britain changed forever when the army of ancient Rome arrived and took over. They built a settlement on the Thames and called it Londinium.

Some local tribes have become friendly with the Romans and helped them to rule the country. But others have been ill-treated by the Romans and decide to teach them a lesson.

▶ *Roman legionaries are a common site on the streets of Roman London.*

✳ *Early Londinium grows up in the area of the City of London. There are also a few buildings by the river and in Southwark.*

✳ *This small town is a port, too. Boats sail up the Thames carrying goods from Rome, and take away grain, lead and tin.*

✳ *Early Londinium is not the capital of Roman Britain. That is Camulodunum, now called Colchester, which is a much bigger military camp.*

✳ *The Roman army builds a bridge across the Thames near modern London Bridge, and they add a road called Watling Street (now Edgware Road) leading north to their other towns.*

Attack!

In 60-61CE Boudica, queen of the Iceni, has led warriors of the Iceni and the Trinovantes in an uprising to drive the Romans out of Britain. They have attacked and destroyed Camulodunum and now they have arrived in Londinium.

The governor in charge of Roman troops realises that he does not have enough men to defend Londinium. He abandons the town and the inhabitants must flee as best they can. Many people will not escape and will be killed by the Celtic warriors. By the end of the attack up to 25,000 people may die, mostly women and children, the old and the ill.

▲ *You can see this Victorian statue of Boudica, queen of the Iceni, near Westminster Bridge.*

Back to the 21st century: Gruesome remains

Deep beneath the streets of London there is grizzly evidence of the terrible events when Londinium was destroyed by Boudica's followers. Achaeologists have found a widespread layer of ash, evidence that the town was burnt to the ground.

Walbrook stream now runs under the streets close to the Bank of England. But in 60–61CE it seems to have been the scene of a bloodthirsty ceremony, when the heads of the dead were thrown into the water, perhaps to please the Celtic gods. The skulls were later found and are now in the Museum of London.

▼ *You can visit sections of surviving Roman wall today.*

Boudica's army were eventually defeated by the Romans, and Londinium was rebuilt, this time with a defensive wall around it. Parts of the wall can still be seen near Tower Hill Tube Station.

◀ *The skulls found in the Walbrook stream, evidence of a London massacre.*

11

Try a taste of Rome

Population: Between 45,000 and 60,000

Welcome to the Roman riverside in Londinium, rebuilt as the new capital of Roman Britain after its destruction by Boudica's warriors. Boats are tied up alongside a wooden quay, and luxury goods all the way from Spain, North Africa and Rome itself are being unloaded. Nearby there are wooden warehouses and small homes for the river workers. In the smarter areas there are luxury townhouses and grand public buildings.

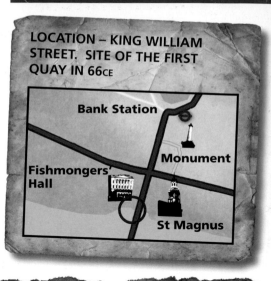
LOCATION – KING WILLIAM STREET. SITE OF THE FIRST QUAY IN 66CE

Bank Station

Monument

Fishmongers' Hall

St Magnus

◉ Visitor's map of Londinium

Uptown Londinium is centred around the Forum, an open meeting square lined with shops and a town hall building called the Basilica. Local people meet here to chat, do business or hear public announcements.

All the things anyone needs to live a comfortable Roman life are now in Londinium, but there is also a large fort full of soldiers, just in case!

Forum

① *There are lots of temples around town. One of them is the Temple of Mithras, a mysterious god popular with soldiers.*

② *An amphitheatre with room for a crowd of 6,000 is under the modern-day Guildhall. Here gladiators fight each other, or fight wild animals.*

③ *Roman public bath remains are dotted around London. One of them is on the corner of modern-day Borough High Street and London Bridge Street.*

④ *Wealthy people live in stone townhouses, called 'domus'. They are decorated with mosaic floors and wall paintings, and have tiled roofs. The governor lives in a grand palace, the best address in town.*

⑤ *Outside Londinium there are farms and country villas where wealthy people go to relax.*

Meet Marcus

Marcus lives down by the riverside and helps to unload the boats. His family are not wealthy so he doesn't go to school, but he learns all about the world from the people who visit the busy quayside.

Today's boat has brought olives from Spain, and Marcus wouldn't mind if you try one. They're packed in pottery pots called amphorae. The boats also bring in luxuries such as wine. In Marcus's time, Londoners are a mixture of local Britons and people from other parts of the Roman Empire. They are, on average, slightly shorter than modern Londoners. They live for between 35 to 45 years and are generally healthy, but often have toothache. We know this from studies done on Roman graves.

A reconstruction of a scene by the quay in Roman times.

Marcus

▶ *A Roman amphora full of olives was found in the Thames and is now in the National Maritime Museum at Greenwich.*

Back to the 21st century: Digging up Londinium

Hidden secrets of Roman Londinium often appear when new buildings are constructed and the ground is dug up. A pot of Roman ointment turned up in Southwark in 2003. It even had Roman fingerprints in the cream. When the pot was re-opened the cream smelled eggy, but nobody knows exactly what it was for. It could be face cream, toothpaste or even a cream to use on sick goats!

The statue head of Mithras, the god of Roman soldiers, is on display at the Museum of London. His worshippers believed that everlasting life came from being spattered with the blood of a bull sacrificed during a secret male-only ceremony.

▼ *Roman statue of Mithras*

▲ *Archaeologists excavate a Roman public baths in Southwark.*

Step into a hut

We're in Anglo-Saxon Lundenwic, and it's very different to how it looked in Roman times. Pigs and chickens are running around thatched wooden buildings in the area we now call Covent Garden. The buildings of Roman Londinium have been left to tumble down, but the river is still busy with boats coming to and from Europe.

Population: 45,000 approx.

LOCATION – FLORAL STREET, COVENT GARDEN

Long Acre
Floral Street
St Martin's Lane
Bedford Street
Covent Garden

◯ What to wear

Before you leave the time machine, you need to dress up as Anglo-Saxon children.

Girls wore a linen underdress and a wool overdress held together by shoulder brooches.

Boys wore linen or wool trousers, a linen tunic and leather shoes, worn with a belt attached to a pouch and a knife.

◯ Your Destination

Roman troops left Britain in 410ce, and warriors from northern Europe began to invade and settle. Eventually a new settlement has appeared to the west of the ruins of Roman Londinium.

Boats still come up the river bringing goods from abroad. In the 8th century, it also brings longships full of fearsome attackers – the Vikings from Scandinavia.

ANGLO-SAXONS IN THE LONDON AREA

Lundenwic - Anglo-Saxon town 2km west of Londinium, in the area between Covent Garden and Trafalgar Square

The area eventually settled by Anglo-Saxons in the ruined Roman Londinium, named Lundenburgh.

Marshy area of Thornhill, where Westminster Abbey is founded.

Billingsgate and Queenhithe, where boats unloaded.

Woods, farms and marshy fields surround London.

Time traveller's timeline ➔

- 410CE The Roman army leaves.
- Late 400s Saxons begin to settle around the River Thames.
- 604 St Paul's Cathedral is founded by King Aethelbert of Kent. Westminster Abbey is also founded around this time.

- 700 The settlement of Lundenwic grows up in the area now called Covent Garden.
- 842 A Danish Viking army lays waste to London in a terrible attack called the 'Great Slaughter'.

- 878 Anglo-Saxon King Alfred defeats the Danes.
- Late 800s King Alfred fortifies the settlement, now called Lundenburgh, against attacks. People move back to the old Roman area.

Meet Edith

Edith is an Anglo-Saxon girl living in Lundenwic. Her mother is busy weaving cloth on a loom inside their thatched hut, and her father has gone to trade the leather shoes he has made for a new knife. Edith's home doesn't have a chimney. Instead smoke drifts up through the roof from the hearth inside.

The family sit and sleep on wooden benches inside their home. The toilet is just a hole in the ground outside.

▲ Anglo-Saxon houses were made of wood and had roofs thatched with reeds.

Edith's father carries a sword which he keeps sharpened, just in case there is a Viking attack. King Alfred is ruling now, but you never know who might try to sail up the river at the dead of night…

Back to the 21st century: Place-name evidence

The Anglo-Saxons did not leave many remains in London, but they did provide us with lots of London place names. Here are a few Anglo-Saxon place names to look out for around London…

THEATRELAND
ALDWYCH WC2
CITY OF WESTMINSTER

◀ 'Aldwych' means 'the old settlement'. It is an important street in London.

Ford – shallow river crossing (eg Catford)

Ham – village (eg Clapham)

Hurst – wooded hill (eg Broadhurst)

Lea – a woodland clearing (eg Wembley)

Hithe – landing place (eg Rotherhithe)

Worth – fenced land (eg Isleworth)

Wych – settlement (eg Aldwych)

Watch the water

The time machine has moved us forward just over a hundred years, and we are standing by the early wooden London Bridge. Screaming Viking warriors line the bridge, aiming their spears towards enemy longboats in the water below. It is another tough day for ordinary Londoners, who must somehow survive yet another battle.

In the early 1000s, Danish Viking warlord Sweyn Forkbeard besieged London. After Forkbeard's death his son Cnut captured London. English King Aethelred had to flee abroad, but now he has returned by ship with reinforcements. His warriors sail up the Thames, attach ropes to London Bridge to pull it down, and re-take London.

▼ *Viking warriors arrive by water in their longboats to attack London.*

Sweyn Forkbeard
(d.1014)

King Aethelred
(d.1016)

Who's in charge?

The struggle between Anglo-Saxons and Vikings went on for many years, making London a war zone for a while. Here are some of the people who fought to control it:

❂ Viking Sweyn Forkbeard, King of Denmark, was King of England for just five weeks before he died. He was a fearsome warrior and an early Christian.

❂ Anglo-Saxon King Aethelred was known as 'the Unready', which means 'ill-advised'. He was constantly at war with the Danes, and fought with his own family, too. He may even have murdered his elder brother.

❂ Cnut eventually reigned for nearly 20 years as the Viking King of England. He was ruthless, but he brought London some much-needed peace.

King Cnut
(d.1035)

Peace for a time

Aethelred's son, Edward the Confessor, will become king in 1042 and set to work on the building of a new abbey at Westminster. The only pictures we have of the early building are on an embroidery called the Bayeux Tapestry, which shows Edward being buried there.

▲ *Edward the Confessor being buried at Westminster Abbey, as shown on the Bayeux Tapestry.*

After Edward's death, King Harold will be crowned at Westminster Abbey. After him, every British monarch will be crowned there, and many will be buried there, too. Anglo-Saxon Londoners will start to hope for peace from invaders at last, as they watch the magnificent abbey being built.

◀ *The magnificent shrine of Edward the Confessor in Westminster Abbey.*

Back to the 21st century: Watery weapons

Vikings fought with axes, swords and spears. A number of these have been found in the River Thames. Perhaps some of them belonged to the Viking warriors who fell in the Thames when Aethelred's warriors pulled down London Bridge.

▶ *Viking weapons found in the River Thames are now on display at the Museum of London.*

Help build a tower

Population: 20,000 approx.

Welcome to a very important building site! A large and impressive stone tower is being built on the north bank of the Thames. Masons are busy cutting stone and labourers are carrying things around the site. There are a couple of soldiers watching, too. It looks as if they are guarding the site, but from what?

LOCATION – TOWER OF LONDON

Tower Hill
Tower Gateway
Tower of London

Conical helmet with nose guard

◀ *A Norman soldier was a new sight in London.*

Chain mail

◉ Meet the new boss

In 1066 Duke William of Normandy invaded England and the last Anglo-Saxon king, Harold, was killed at the Battle of Hastings. William brought over his French-speaking troops and nobles, who were now in charge of the country. Not everybody was happy with the new regime, so revolution was never far away.

◉ Your Destination

Once William won at Hastings, he marched his army north to London, where he was crowned on Christmas Day in Westminster Abbey.

He has set about controlling the town and the surrounding countryside, building a large high tower that everybody can see for miles around as a symbol of power. One day this will be called the Tower of London.

✣ When William arrived, his troops burned the countryside around London. Realising they couldn't hold out, Londoners invited him into the city.

✣ When William was crowned, his soldiers outside Westminster Abbey set fire to buildings when they heard shouting from inside the church. It was, in fact, the people inside acclaiming William as king.

✣ William has realised that the support of London is important to him, so he has granted the city a charter confirming the rights of the people there. It is an important step towards London becoming the capital.

▲ *This view of early medieval London shows the location of the Tower of London.*

Meet Osric

Osric is a local boy who is helping to build the White Tower. This is a tall, stone, square building called a 'keep', surrounded by walls, ditches and palisades. Nobody in Britain has ever seen a building like it!

The masons are the most important workers on the site. They have been brought over from France, and Osric finds it hard to understand their French. The rest of the workmen on the site have come from the countryside around.

Osric lives nearby with his family, in a crowded street of narrow houses. None of the homes have running water or toilets, so the narrow roads of London are dirty and smelly.

Osric has brought some bread and cheese with him to eat today. Wealthy lords eat far better, tucking into animals such as deer that they have hunted. The Normans have brought some new foods to England, including pheasants and types of pear.

▼ *We know the White Tower was begun around 1075 because scientists have worked out the dates of tree rings in wood used to build it.*

Back to the 21st century: Norman architecture

The Tower of London has grown much bigger since Norman times, but the original part, the White Tower (above), can still be seen. It has been used as a prison, a treasure house and a place to hide in times of trouble.

The Normans introduced a new kind of architecture to England, called Romanesque. It had round arches, buttresses that supported stone walls and stone ceiling ribs called vaults to support the weight of a stone roof. The beautiful chapel inside the White Tower has simple rounded Romanesque arches.

▼ *The Chapel of St John inside the White Tower may have been brightly painted originally.*

Bow to the mayor

You are back in the City of London, but the roads are much busier because the town is growing. A group of merchants are walking by, wearing luxury robes edged with fox fur. They seem important, and passers-by bow and move to let them pass. "That's the Lord Mayor and his friends," grins a young man. "You don't want to upset them if you want to keep a job around here!"

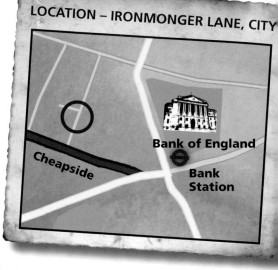

LOCATION – IRONMONGER LANE, CITY

Cheapside

Bank of England

Bank Station

What to wear

What Londoners are wearing depends on how rich they are. You could choose the clothes of a merchant, a wealthy lady, a monk or nun, or a peasant. Peasants look much the same as they did in Norman times.

A wealthy lady wore a long embroidered gown over a woollen smock and stockings, with a headdress.

A merchant wore a long thick robe and woollen stockings with fashionable leather shoes.

Your Destination

Edward I is ruling England in 1300, one of a new dynasty (family) of rulers called the Plantagenets. London hasn't always been peaceful during the last hundred years. It is growing in size to become England's wealthy centre of government and business.

❋ The King has a palace at Westminster, and his advisors meet at Westminster Hall. He and his nobles are in charge of government.

❋ Over in the old city, different types of craftsmen work in different areas. For instance, fishmongers are based around Old Fish Street.

❋ New monasteries and convents (in red) are founded around London during this period. Monks and nuns spend their days working and praying.

❋ The City (in brown) is still surrounded by walls, and travellers have to pass through gatehouses to get in and out. The gates are shut from dusk to dawn.

▲ By 1300, London has grown, mainly on the north bank of the river.

Meet Will

Will is the young man watching the Lord Mayor go by. He's there because the city's metal workers are based in the area, and he is learning the business. Trades in London are organised into guilds, with their own strict rules.

Will is an apprentice to a master craftsman, and he will take years to learn his job well enough to be accepted as a guild member. Only then will he be allowed to practise his trade.

King John granted the City of London a Charter in 1216. It confirmed in writing the many rights of Londoners.

▲ *The Charter of King John granted the right to elect the Lord Mayor from the Masters of the guilds.*

▲ *Graves of knights in the Temple Church*

Fighting monks

The Knights Templars were a group of fighting monks who had a headquarters in London. They fought crusades, or religious wars, in the Middle East and raised money for their campaigns through banking. Their Temple Church still exists today. It is round, representing the Church of the Holy Sepulchre in Jerusalem, the site where Jesus is said to be buried.

Back to the 21st century: The Lord Mayor's Show

The Lord Mayor is still elected from the Livery Companies (the modern name for guilds) in the City of London. The centre of government in the City is the Guildhall, first built in medieval times.

Every year in November the Lord Mayor's Show – a procession through the City of London – is held. It dates back 800 years, to the time when each new medieval Lord Mayor was expected to go to Westminster to swear allegiance to the King.

There is also a Mayor of London, elected by the people of London. The Mayor is a political leader, responsible for running the whole of the capital.

▲ *A Lord Mayor rides in his golden ceremonial carriage during the Lord Mayor's Show.*

Buy a pie

If you're hungry, you're in luck. The time machine has landed in medieval London's busiest market at Cheapside, and there is plenty of food to buy. London has been through some terrible times since we last visited, however. Around a third of its people died suddenly between 1348 and 1349, killed by a plague called the Black Death. A few of the oldest people in the market remember those awful days.

▲ *Workers dumped carts full of dead bodies into plague pits during the Black Death.*

The plague strikes

Nobody knew it at the time, but the plague was carried by fleas that came into the country on black rats that lived on ships arriving from abroad. The fast-spreading disease soon ripped through London, where people were crowded into small houses in narrow filthy streets. Whole families were wiped out within days and nobody was spared loss. Even the king's daughter died. There were too many bodies to bury separately, so they were piled into huge open plague pits. Medieval plague pit sites we know of include Charterhouse Square, Artillery Lane in Shoreditch and East Smithfield. New ones sometimes come to light when building sites are dug around London.

◎ Your Destination

Thankfully, the Black Death is no longer a problem and it's safe to walk the streets again. Everybody buys their food in London's street markets. The names of the roads around Cheapside – such as Milk Street, Honey Lane and Poultry – provide clues to the food sold there. There is a meat market at nearby Smithfield.

A medieval market

❋ *Salting and drying is the only way of preserving food, as there is no refrigeration. There is no way of growing crops all year round, so all the food at the market is in season or preserved.*

❋ *Ordinary people use root vegetables such as parsnips, beetroots and carrots, to make a broth called pottage, with onions, beans and lentils.*

❋ *Wealthy people prefer lots of meat and fish, so they often lack vitamins in their diet, and suffer from bad skin, rotting teeth and bone diseases such as rickets.*

Trouble in town

London Bridge is an important London entry route at this time. It is lined with shops and houses, and the road is often blocked by carts and crowds. Shop signs hang high up on the buildings so as not to bash the heads of the riders on their horses below. Meanwhile the piers under the bridge make the river water run very fast, like rapids, and boat passengers are regularly drowned trying to get through.

London Bridge is often the scene of important events, including riots. In 1381 workers marched on London, demanding new rights. They crossed the bridge and burnt some of the houses on it, but at Smithfield their leader, Wat Tyler, was stabbed by the Lord Mayor, and the rebellion ended. Executed traitors have their heads stuck on poles on the bridge, as an example for all to see.

▲ *A medieval impression of the death of Wat Tyler in Smithfield in 1381.*

Back to the 21st century: London markets

You can visit all kinds of different street and covered markets in modern London, some of them dating back centuries. Smithfield meat market and Borough Market in Southwark both date to medieval times. You cannot visit the old bridge, though. It was pulled down in the 1800s.

Today's markets have similar features to the old ones, though they are not necessarily in the same place. Outdoor stalls are piled with goods, and the stallholders sometimes call out to advertise what they are selling.

Different markets sell different things. For instance, at Borough Market you can buy many types of food, whereas at Petticoat Lane you can buy clothing.

▶ *Vegetables have been sold at London's Borough Market since the 1200s.*

Have fun at a feast

Population: 60,000 approx.

The time machine has landed at Hampton Court Palace and there's a royal feast going on in the Great Hall. Hundreds of noisy courtiers are tucking into roast meat, pies and puddings. At the far end of the room King Henry VIII is sitting with his new young wife, Jane Seymour. Be very careful not to upset him because he could send you to the Tower!

LOCATION – HAMPTON COURT

Bushy Park

Hampton Court Station

Hampton Court Park

◯ What to wear

Choose an outfit that ordinary London children would wear in 1536. If you were wealthy you would wear much finer clothes.

Girls wore a woollen bodice and skirt over a linen shift (underdress), a linen cap called a coif and leather shoes.

Boys wore a woollen tunic over baggy linen shirt, woollen breeches, hose (long socks) and leather shoes.

◯ Your Destination

The Tudor dynasty now rules England and Wales and owns several royal palaces dotted around the capital. In 1536 there is a plague outbreak in London during the hot summer months, so King Henry has taken the whole court upriver to Hampton Court Palace. Several hundred people have arrived, and they all need to be fed twice a day!

▲ **Aerial view of Hampton Court Palace.**

✥ *Cooking fires burn continually in the palace kitchens. Some of the kitchen servants are children, who help the cooks by doing jobs such as keeping the fires going.*

✥ *Henry does not need to travel along bumpy roads to get to Hampton Court. He is rowed in luxury aboard his royal barge.*

✥ *Hampton Court Palace was built by Henry's advisor, Thomas Wolsey, but Henry seized it for himself. He has spent vast amounts of money on improvements.*

✥ *Henry's happiness will be short-lived. His third wife Jane Seymour will give birth to a son in 1537, but will also die here at the palace.*

⬤ Time traveller's timeline – the Tudor Dynasty ------------➤

- **1485–1509** Henry VII becomes king by winning a civil war called the Wars of the Roses.
- **1509–1547** Henry VIII has six wives, beheading two of them.

- **1547–1553** Edward VI becomes king when he is nine years old and dies at the age of 15.
- **1553–1558** Mary I, the eldest daughter of Henry VIII, rules.

- **1558–1603** Elizabeth I, the youngest daughter of Henry VIII, rules.

Palace life

King Henry has added all kinds of features to his new palace at Hampton Court. He likes sport, so he has had a tennis court built to play real tennis, an early version of modern tennis. He holds jousting tournaments and hunts in nearby Bushy Park. Because so many people live at court, daily life is governed by a set of strict rules called the Ordinances of Eltham.

Henry adds up-to-the minute luxuries such as an astronomical clock that displays star signs as well as the time. He has had a toilet block fitted called the Great House of Easement. Twenty-eight people can use these toilets at the same time, and the waste is washed through drains into the Thames.

◀ *The elaborate gatehouse of Hampton Court Palace*

⬤ Back to the 21st century: Thames river trips

You can still travel by boat to Hampton Court, just as Henry did. The palace retains many Tudor features, including the kitchens, the real tennis court and the astronomical clock.

Anyone who upset a Tudor monarch was taken the opposite way along the river, to prison and possible execution in the Tower of London. You can still see Traitors' Gate, the water gate where prisoners entered the Tower by boat, sometimes never to be seen again.

▲ *Traitors' Gate at the Tower of London*

Walk Shakespeare's way

You are standing on the south shore of the River Thames. The stately gilded barge gliding by carries Queen Elizabeth I to her palace at Greenwich. Meanwhile people are hurrying excitedly past you on their way to see a play at the Globe, one of the district's new theatres.

The south bank of the Thames is the hot party spot in Tudor London!

LOCATION – BANKSIDE

Blackfriars   St Paul's

Tate Modern

The Globe theatre

Southwark

◄ *A replica of the* Golden Hind, *the ship Sir Francis Drake used to sail around the world.*

Something missing

London has grown four times bigger in Elizabeth's lifetime and is becoming one of the world's busiest ports. It is getting more crowded and smellier too. However monks, so long a part of London life, are now gone because Henry VIII closed all the monasteries in his kingdom.

◯ Your Destination

You are in an place called Bankside. It is the part of London where people come to have fun. There are theatres, taverns and 'pits' – buildings for staging fights between dogs and bulls or bears. Playwright William Shakespeare works here, at the Globe theatre.

① It costs a penny to get a lift in a row-ing boat across the Thames to Bankside.

② Bankside has lots of gardens and ponds, where fish are kept to eat.

③ People come here to visit the taverns. It's a drunken noisy place sometimes!

④ The Bishop of Winchester owns lots of the buildings in this area. People rent their homes and shops from him.

⑤ Near the bear-baiting pit there are ponds where bears are allowed to swim.

⑥ Farm fields were not far up the road.

Meet John

John is 12 and he is apprenticed (in training) with an apothecary who makes herbal cures. He comes from a poor family so he doesn't go to school. Spend the day with him...

6am Time to get up. John lives with the apothecary's family above their shop. He sleeps on a mattress made of sack and stuffed with straw. He eats bread and cheese for breakfast.

10am John goes to get some shopping for his mistress. He narrowly avoids tripping over the farm animals wandering around the narrow muddy lanes. A rat leaps over his foot and makes him jump!

10.30am Somebody throws their slops out onto the street and John gets splashed with dirty water. Hopefully it's not the contents of a chamberpot!

11am Time for lunch – boiled rabbit and onions today, with some ale to drink. John eats off a wooden plate with a spoon and a knife. He's never seen a fork.

2pm John is allowed a big treat today. He goes with his master to see a play at the Globe. They stand near the stage, in the cheapest part of the theatre, so when it starts to rain they get wet.

5pm John and his master go to the Falcon Tavern, where a noisy tableful of men are laughing and arguing. John's master says they are actors from the local theatres.

8pm Once it gets dark John goes to bed, by candlelight.

Tudor coins

Back to the 21st century: Shakespeare's Globe

Today you can go to Southwark on the south bank of the Thames to visit a reconstruction of Shakespeare's Globe theatre and watch a play there. The new theatre is built not far from where the old one stood.

People who stood in the front were called 'groundlings'. They were very close to the actors and were probably a nuisance at times. They got wet when it rained, and the actors sometimes complained that they smelled.

A play being rehearsed in the Globe and (inset above) the exterior of the theatre.

In modern plays you will see women on stage, but in Shakespeare's time women were banned from acting and all the female parts were played by boys in women's clothes.

There was no big scenery on stage, but there were props – objects such as a fake tree or a throne. The actors wore Tudor clothes, as shown left.

London kills a king

It is a freezing cold January morning and a large crowd is gathered in Whitehall outside the Banqueting House, huddling expectantly around a wooden platform on which stands an execution block. The crowd is hushed as a man is brought out under guard. When the axe falls on his neck people gasp. King Charles I has been executed!

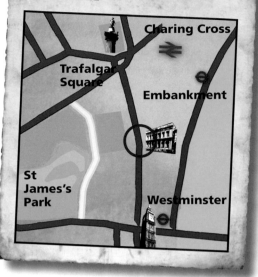

LOCATION – BANQUETING HOUSE, WHITEHALL

Charing Cross

Trafalgar Square

Embankment

St James's Park

Westminster

What to wear

Before leaving your time machine choose an outfit that people might wear in 1649. As always, how a person dressed in London depended on how wealthy they were.

Women wore a long woollen skirt and a short bodice with long sleeves over linen underclothes.

Men wore knee-length breeches, a short jacket over a linen shirt and a broad-brimmed hat.

Your Destination

The Banqueting House is part of Whitehall Palace. Charles is a member of the ruling Stuart dynasty, but Parliament has been trying to limit King Charles' power and increase its own. This has resulted in violent civil war across the country. In addition, serious religious arguments between Protestant Puritans, Anglicans and Roman Catholics have caused trouble across the nation.

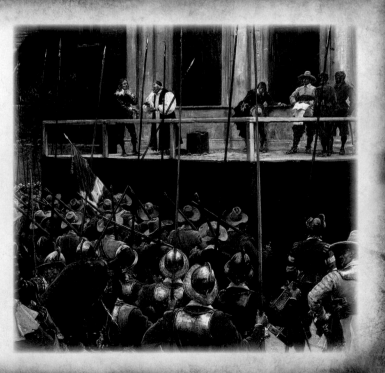

▶ *This painting of the scene shows Charles (far left) speaking to Archbishop Juxon just before the execution.*

8

Time traveller's timeline - the Stuart Dynasty to 1649 - - - - - - →

- 1603 James VI of Scotland inherits the crown to become King James I of England and Scotland.

- 1627 James dies and his son Charles becomes King Charles I.

- 1642 Charles I goes to war against Parliament. Many bloody battles ensue.

- 1645 The critical Battle of Naseby ends in defeat for King Charles.

- 1649 After a trial, King Charles is executed in London for 'Waging war against Parliament'.

A useful time-travelling map In 1616 Dutchman Nicolas Visscher made a beautiful engraved view of London, shown here.

Old St Paul's Cathedral

The Thames is London's highway and is always busy with water traffic.

London Bridge with its shops — and traitors' heads stuck up over the gateway.

Southwark, with its gardens, taverns and theatres

St Mary Overie church (now Southwark Cathedral)

Ships crowd the river below London Bridge.

Back to the 21st century: Whitehall and Westminster

Whitehall today is a busy street lined with government and military buildings. You can still visit the Banqueting House (the last part of Whitehall Palace still standing) and see the spot where King Charles was executed. The Banqueting House was built for elaborate court parties called masques, when nobles dressed up, acted out stories set to music, danced and drank all night long.

Parliament still meets and makes laws nearby at Westminster, as it has done since the 1400s. The Prime Minister lives at 10 Downing Street, a street located just off Whitehall.

▲ *The Banqueting House*

Fire!

The air is black with choking smoke and flames are shooting up into the sky. Luckily you are on board a barge in the river, so you are safe from the fire raging through the old city. On the shore, desperate Londoners are trying to get their belongings into boats or just abandoning everything they own to save themselves.

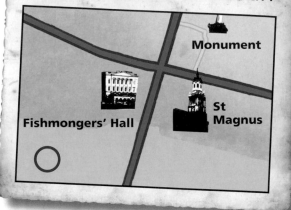

LOCATION – ON BOARD A BARGE IN THE RIVER, LOOKING AT THE BURNING CITY

Monument

Fishmongers' Hall

St Magnus

Your Destination

PUDDING LANE EC3

The fire started early in the morning at the premises of the King's baker, Thomas Farynor, in Pudding Lane. Fanned by strong winds, it has spread quickly through the wooden thatched buildings. Burning embers, driven by the wind, carry the fire between the narrow streets.

There is no fire brigade, only local militia (soldiers), and they don't have any firefighting equipment. The best defence is to pull down houses in the path of the fire, but the flames often move too fast for this.

A terrible time

The Great Fire of London comes after 18 months of hell for London. In 1665 plague spread through the city, and nearly 70,000 people died in the outbreak. Carts full of bodies have been trundling through the streets, accompanied by the ringing of a plague bell, a signal to bring out the dead.

▶ *An original plague bell, now in the Museum of London.*

From the Diary of Samuel Pepys:

"...all over the Thames, with one's face in the wind you were almost burned with a shower of firedrops...When we could endure no more upon the water, we (went) to a little alehouse on the Bankside...and there stayed till it was dark almost and saw the fire grow...We stayed till, it being darkish, we saw the fire as only one entire arch of fire from this to the other side of the bridge, and in a bow up the hill, for an arch of above a mile long. It made me weep to see it."

Samuel Pepys, famous diary-writer of the time.

After the fire

The fire leaves four-fifths of the City of London destroyed: 13,000 homes, 87 churches, 44 livery halls and the Royal Exchange burn to the ground. The old cathedral of St Paul's goes up in flames and its lead roof melts. Rivers of molten lead flow off the building into the street.

Although only ten people die in the flames, we know that people are dying in the refugee camps that are set up on the outskirts of town.

▲ *A painting of the Great Fire devastating the old City and creeping over London Bridge.*

Charles II

King Charles II goes to address 10,000 refugees living as best they can on parkland in Moorfields. He encourages them to leave London and move elsewhere for good.

People think that foreigners are to blame for starting the fire, and mobs rampage through the town, murdering any foreigners they find. A French watchmaker eventually confesses to starting the fire, and is hanged, but it is later discovered that he was out of the country at the time. Nobody knows why he confessed to something he didn't do.

⬤ Back to the 21st century: The Monument

The Monument marks the spot where the Great Fire of London started. It is 61m (202ft) high, exactly the distance between its position and the spot where the fire is thought to have begun. It was designed by architect Sir Christopher Wren to celebrate the rebuilding of London.

You can climb to the top for a panoramic view of the City, or you can see the view on a webcam at the bottom.

▶ *The Monument is topped by a golden urn of fire.*

All change

A group of people are gathered in the June sun on the site of old St Paul's. One of them is fixing a stone in place, watched intently by a man in a frock coat and wig, carrying a roll of paper under his arm. He is Sir Christopher Wren, King Charles' chosen architect. Already the designer of many London churches, he is carrying the plans for a new cathedral with a beautiful giant dome. Building starts today.

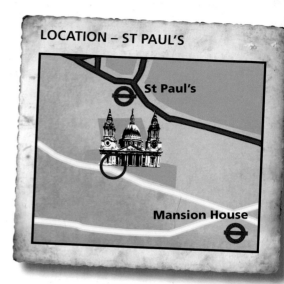

LOCATION – ST PAUL'S

St Paul's

Mansion House

○ Your Destination

After the Great Fire the City is re-growing more or less on the old street plan. But the new buildings are stone, not wood, and the streets themselves are wider.

Grand buildings are being erected in a decorative luxury style called 'baroque', decorated with fine paintings and stone carvings. Wealthy nobles are choosing to move away from the old City to grand new houses in Whitehall and St James.

❊ *Christopher Wren has had to change his plans for St Paul's several times, to please Church and court officials.*

❊ *The new cathedral will be a busy building site for years. It won't be ready to open until 1697. By the time it is fully finished in 1711 it will cost the equivalent of £147 million.*

❊ *The dome will be one of the highest in the world. Inside will be the Whispering Gallery, 259 steps up from the ground. A whisper on one side of the gallery can be heard all the way round the dome on the other side.*

Sir Christopher Wren

▲ *The huge dome of St Paul's dominates the City of London in this 18th century painting.*

❊ *Christopher Wren will eventually be buried in his cathedral masterpiece. His tomb will have a Latin inscription which, translated, reads: "If you seek a memorial, look around you."*

Meet Annabel

Annabel is the daughter of a wealthy aristocrat and lives in a grand new home built by the river near Whitehall. Her mother has helped her pick out a smart dress as today she will be travelling by boat to Greenwich with her father. They are both very interested in science and excited by a new building the King has ordered Wren to build there – an observatory for studying the stars.

In the late 1600s people are becoming more interested in scientific discoveries and mathematics. Astronomers at the Royal Observatory hope to discover new ways for sailors to accurately chart their position by the stars.

Britain relies on its ships and sailors for trade and exploration. On the river journey, Annabel and her father will pass many sailing ships being loaded and unloaded at the docksides.

Because Annabel is an aristocrat's daughter, she has been taught at home by a tutor. Wealthy boys also get an education, but poor London children get no schooling, and are expected to work from an early age.

◀ *This 17th-century reflecting telescope. now at the Royal Observatory, belonged to scientist Sir Isaac Newton.*

Back to the 21st century: Greenwich and St Paul's

Greenwich still has some of the Stuart buildings that Annabel would have seen. You can visit the National Maritime Museum in Charles II's Royal Naval College and see the original Royal Observatory, too. At the Observatory you can step across the meridian, the line which separates the eastern and western hemispheres of the world.

The dome of St Paul's Cathedral is still a major feature of the City of London skyline. You can climb stairs up to the dome and whisper across the Whispering Gallery to a friend standing on the opposite side.

▶ *The west front of St Paul's Cathedral*

Go grand

Population: 740,000 approx.

Welcome to Vauxhall Pleasure Gardens. There are thousands of people here, walking around the pathways or eating in the supper boxes. The visitors are dressed in their finest clothes, and many are hoping to catch a glimpse of the celebrities of the day. An orchestra is tuning up, and there is an air of excitement. It is going to be a very exciting London night!

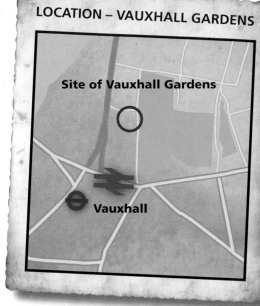

LOCATION – VAUXHALL GARDENS

Site of Vauxhall Gardens

Vauxhall

What to wear

The throne has passed to the Hanoverians, a family from Germany. Four British Hanoverian kings will be called George, so the era you have now arrived in is known as the Georgian period of British history.

Men's clothing was colourful, with long jackets worn over waistcoats and breeches.

Women wore bonnets tied under the chin and long dresses over stiffened corsets. Cane hoops held out the skirt of the dress.

Your Destination

London has grown in size and wealth, thanks to increasing sea trade with the rest of the world. Wealthy people want to spend their money and be seen in fashionable places.

Nowhere is more fashionable than Vauxhall Pleasure Gardens, and tonight there is a dress rehearsal for the new Royal Fireworks music, by celebrated composer Handel.

▶ *The Grand Walk at Vauxhall in 1751 was a place to see and be seen.*

✳ *The gardens are open to anyone for an entrance fee of 1 shilling. The most exclusive spots are the dining boxes where the well-to-do can eat supper and hear the orchestra.*

✳ *Around the pathways you can see art and statues. When it gets dark, over a thousand oil lamps are lit at the same time.*

✳ *Handel has been commissioned by King George II to write the Music for the Royal Fireworks as a background for a big display. This dress rehearsal has proved hugely popular, and 12,000 people have turned up!*

GEORGIAN TIMES – 1714 TO 1837

New buildings, new style

Much of the area between the City and Whitehall is now filling in with new buildings, many designed in a grand new style called 'Palladian'.

▲ Built in the 1770s, Somerset House – one of the first purpose-built government office buildings in the world – displays many grand Palladian features.

Palladian style

Look out for these Palladian features on London streets:

• front entrances that have stone columns and look like temple fronts from ancient Greece or Rome;

• sash windows, a new-ish invention;

• rows of houses in squares, crescents and circles.

• Somerset House is a good example of the new Palladian style. It was once a Tudor mansion but it was beginning to fall down. It was rebuilt as grand government offices.

Back to the 21st century: Grand v. rustic

Many Palladian buildings still stand in the West End of London, lining elegant squares and crescents.

Somerset House is a centre for the arts. In summer 55 fountains flow in its square and in winter, the courtyard is turned into an ice rink. Georgian crowds would have loved it!

Vauxhall Pleasure Gardens no longer exist, but there are plenty of other parks where visitors can stroll. The Georgian royal family had their own peaceful park at Kew, and you can follow in their footsteps by visiting Queen Charlotte's cottage in Kew Gardens, a thatched cottage built for the wife of George III, so that she and her servants could take picnics there on park walks.

▲ Queen Charlotte's cottage at Kew was built in a rustic, not a grand, style.

Watch your purse

You are once more in a crowd of thousands and there seems to be a party atmosphere, but look up the road and you will see a set of gallows – a wooden frame with a noose hanging from it. This is Tyburn tree, in the west of London, and people have gathered here to see a slow agonising death. A cart rattles towards the gallows, carrying a condemned man. His crime? Cutting down a tree to provide firewood for his family.

▲ A hanging at Tyburn, as depicted by the artist William Hogarth (1697–1764). Public hangings were a rowdy day out for ordinary Londoners.

Crime doesn't pay

Many people are living in grinding poverty in the 1700s, and so turn to crime. In response, the government has made over 150 offences punishable by death – including pickpocketing anything worth more than a shilling, being out at night with a blackened face, cutting down trees and stealing from a rabbit warren. Some criminals are transported to American penal colonies. In 1787 they are sent to penal colonies in Australia for the first time.

Your Destination

Hangings at Tyburn take place every six weeks, on Mondays. The prisoner is taken by cart from Newgate Prison, west across town to Tyburn. This is where the expression 'gone west' comes from, meaning 'finished'.

The cart procession can take up to two hours, and crowds line the route cheering and jeering. There have been several rescue attempts and attacks on prisoners over the years, and the atmosphere is highly charged.

① At Newgate, prisoners are released from their chains and put on a cart, often sitting on their own coffin.

② The cart moves down Snow Hill to High Holborn. Sometimes onlookers rent the upper storeys of houses to get a better look at the prisoners.

③ At St Giles, site of the worst slums in London, they stop at an inn and are given a final pint of ale. The expression 'on the wagon' comes from this time, probably because the hangman stayed on the cart and didn't drink.

④ Once at the gallows prisoners are allowed to speak to the crowd. Then a noose is put around each neck and the cart is driven off, leaving them to die by strangulation.

Marble Arch

Newgate

A life of crime

Some of the most famous criminals of the 1700s are highwaymen who rob wealthy travellers on lonely roads (below). Hounslow Heath is a well-known highwayman's haunt at this time. Some highwaymen became celebrity anti-heroes – 200,000 people turned up to see Jack Sheppard hanged in 1724.

In the early 1700s there is no official police force. The authorities pay for information and capture, and informers called 'thief-takers' make a living that way. In 1748 the Fielding brothers set up an office and hire thief-takers to investigate crimes and track down culprits. Their men are called the Bow Street Runners and become the first official law enforcers on London's streets.

Back to the 21st century: Crime and punishment

There is a small round plaque on a traffic island in Marble Arch, said to mark the spot of the Tyburn tree. You can visit an original London prison cell taken from Wellclose Prison, in Tower Hamlets, and rebuilt at the Museum of London.

Prisoners found guilty of crimes at sea were hanged at Execution Dock in Wapping. The gallows were placed just above the low tide mark of the Thames, and the bodies were not cut down until three tides had washed over them. A mocked-up set of pirate gallows now stands at The Prospect of Whitby pub.

▲ *The prison cell in the Museum of London still has lots of graffiti scratched on its walls by prisoners.*

Wave a flag

It's a beautiful June day and we're going to join around 350,000 people lining the route between Buckingham Palace and Westminster Abbey to watch Queen Victoria on her way to be crowned. Her reign will last 63 years and will see London grow bigger than she could ever imagine, but for now this young 18-year-old can only gasp at the size of the cheering crowds.

Population: 2 million approx.

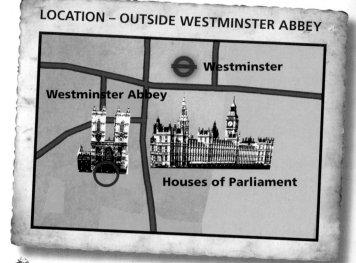

LOCATION – OUTSIDE WESTMINSTER ABBEY

Westminster

Westminster Abbey

Houses of Parliament

What to wear

You will be dressed as wealthy children to see the Coronation. If you were a poor London child you might be in rags and bare feet.

Girls wore a long dress with a sash, stockings and button-up boots.

Boys wore fancy trousers, a cravat, shirt and a tight, fitted jacket.

✳ *The peers (Lords) are all here to touch the Queen's crown and kiss her hand. One very fat Lord falls over and rolls down the stairs in front of her.*

Your Destination

Many people have arrived in London on the new railways, to join in the celebration. Meanwhile, events are being held around the country and even people in prison will get extra food and drink today.

Queen Victoria

✳ *It will take one and a half hours for Victoria to reach the Abbey from Buckingham Palace, where she was woken at 4am by the sound of guns being fired.*

✳ *At the ceremony the church officials get confused, and one of them forces the official ring onto the wrong finger. It will be painful for Queen Victoria to get it off later!*

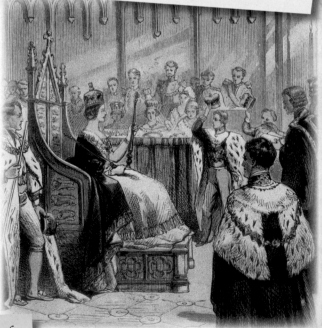

▲ *Queen Victoria at her coronation, surrounded by peers.*

Victorian hotspots

✳ *London will grow hugely during Victoria's long reign, and many new buildings will appear.*

✳ *Victorian London stinks of sewage until engineer James Bazalgette builds a giant network of tunnels and pipes to divert it from the city.*

✳ *Fire has destroyed the old Houses of Parliament, and during Victoria's reign a new one is built (below). The giant bell inside St Stephen's Tower gets the nickname Big Ben.*

✳ *As London grows, so do its crowded slums (above). Poor Londoners and refugees from around the world try to survive as best they can in terrible conditions.*

✳ *Trafalgar Square is built to commemorate Admiral Nelson's defeat of the French and Spanish navies in 1805. His statue is three times life-size. The lions in the square are made of metal from old battleship guns.*

✳ *In 1861 Queen Victoria's husband, Prince Albert, dies. The Albert Hall, the Albert Memorial and the Victoria and Albert Museum are all named after him.*

◉ Back to the 21st century: Sight-seeing

The grandest home in Victorian London was Buckingham Palace, where the current Queen Elizabeth II still lives. You can see the state carriages there, still used today.

Trafalgar Square is a meeting place for Londoners and is surrounded by grand Victorian buildings. On New Year's Eve crowds gather in the square to celebrate. You can take a bus tour from the square to hear the history of the slums that grew up during the Victorian period.

▲ *One of the state carriages on display in the Royal Mews at Buckingham Palace.*

Ride the rails

You are standing by an iron pillar next to a giant steaming, puffing metal machine. Can you see a small man in a tall top hat, waving a cigar around as he points things out to admiring onlookers? He is the noted engineer Isambard Kingdom Brunel at the opening of his new masterpiece, Paddington Station. He has made it look very grand, like an iron cathedral, because it is built to house the very latest exciting new London development – the steam railway.

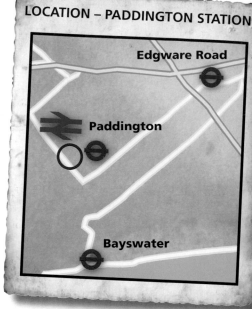

LOCATION – PADDINGTON STATION

Edgware Road

Paddington

Bayswater

Travel by train

New inventions are changing life in London, none more so than the railways. Not everyone was keen at first. Some even thought that travelling fast on a train might make it impossible to breathe! Now, however, goods and passengers are travelling without harm.

✳ Other new stations around London, such as Waterloo, St Pancras and Victoria, link London to different parts of the country and have similar cathedral-like buildings.

◎ Your Destination

In 1836 the first passenger train ran from London to Greenwich. Since then, new stations and lines have opened up one by one. Everyone is amazed by how quickly they can travel about. Railways are so much quicker than ferries or coaches.

✳ The most comfortable way to travel on a steam train is in first class where there are padded seats and plenty of oil lamps.

▶ A scene in a Victorian first-class railway carriage.

✳ In second or third class there might be uncomfortable wooden benches and only a few lamps.

✳ In any section of the train, you might get covered in dirty smuts from the train's coal smoke if you open a window.

✳ By the end of the 1800s nearly all the towns in Britain will have railway stations, and the railways make it easier to travel abroad, too.

✳ Fresh goods such as fruit arrive in London quickly from around the country now, as well as mail and newspapers.

Knocking down. Building up.

To make way for the stations and railway lines, many London slums have been knocked down and their tenants evicted (sent from their homes). For instance, around 3,000 people were evicted to make way for the railway line into Fenchurch Street Station.

London streets have got very busy with horse-drawn cabs or trams carrying passengers between the different railway stations. To solve the problem, the first underground railway will be opened in 1863 between Paddington and Farringdon Street.

The first underground steam trains will run along shallow cuttings with roofs. The stations and tunnels will be filled with stinking smoke from the trains!

▼ *VIPs rode in open wagons when the London Underground opened in 1863.*

Back to the 21st century: On the move

▼ *The glass-panelled roof has been part of St Pancras Station since it was opened in 1877.*

London's Victorian railway stations are still being used, though the railway network is much bigger. Look out for Victorian decorative ironwork, such as curls and arch shapes made of iron, next time you travel to a big London station. In addition, about 2.5 million people use the London Underground, the 'Tube', every single day.

At the London Museum of Transport you can see some original trains and trams from Victorian times, as well as transport through London's history.

See some wonders

You are standing outside a beautiful building decorated with brown tiles, unlike anything seen before in London. It is a new museum of natural history and inside there are many amazing natural treasures. A group of Victorians are by the entrance, with impressive beards and smart top hats. They are the important scientists of the day.

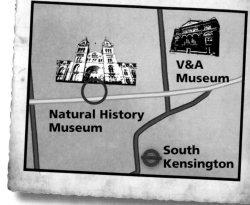

LOCATION – OUTSIDE THE NATURAL HISTORY MUSEUM, IN ALBERTOPOLIS AREA

V&A Museum

Natural History Museum

South Kensington

▲ *The Great Exhibition was held in a huge glass building called the Crystal Palace.*

The Great Exhibition

This area of town is called Albertopolis after Prince Albert, husband of Queen Victoria. He raised the money for the museums by organising a giant show, the Great Exhibition, in 1851, showcasing science and the arts. He died suddenly in 1861 and the heartbroken Queen Victoria has worn black ever since his death.

Your Destination

Everywhere you go in this area you will find Albert's name. Albertopolis has the Victoria and Albert Museum, the Royal Albert Hall and the Albert Memorial.

✻ *The British Museum (Natural History) is built in a style called 'Gothic', used to build medieval cathedrals. People say the new museum looks like a 'cathedral of nature'.*

✻ *Scientists have become fascinated by dinosaurs, though nobody knows exactly what they looked like or when they lived. At the Great Exhibition Richard Owen and other important scientists were even invited to eat dinner inside a model dinosaur.*

▲ *The Victorians founded the Natural History Museum because they were interested in science and nature.*

See the world (in London)

Victorians are fascinated by live animals and plants, as well as old specimens.

London Zoo opened to the public in 1847, and in 1850 it received the first ever hippopotamus seen in Britain. He was called Obaysch and he was a huge sensation, attracting 10,000 visitors a day.

Kew Gardens becomes a popular tourist attraction when giant greenhouses are built to house plants from all over the globe.

▼ *The Palm House at Kew Gardens was built to house huge trees. It was inspired by the Crystal Palace.*

▶ *Bears were also popular with visitors to London Zoo. The animals had wooden poles to climb on and visitors were allowed to feed them buns.*

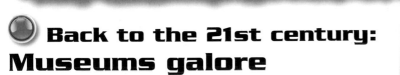

Back to the 21st century: Museums galore

Now people usually call Albertopolis Kensington, but its wonderful museums are still there for everyone to visit.

The Victoria and Albert Museum has beautiful craft objects and art. The Natural History Museum has thousands of exhibits and is especially famous for its dinosaurs. At the Science Museum you can find out how things work, and see all kinds of machines.

Kew Gardens has the world's largest collection of living plants, with over 30,000 in its care.

▲ *Part of an art exhibition at the Victoria and Albert Museum.*

Curtain up

There's an excited crowd outside the New Gaiety Theatre in London's West End. Smartly dressed guests are arriving to see the first night of a new musical comedy, and even the King and Queen are here. The theatre is all the rage in Edwardian London, the name given to the time when Edward VII reigned. He is known for his love of partying around town!

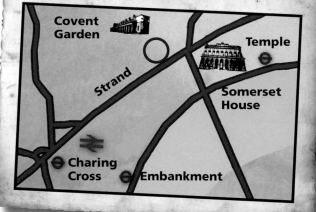

LOCATION: NEW GAIETY THEATRE EASTERN END OF THE STRAND

Covent Garden

Temple

Strand

Somerset House

Charing Cross

Embankment

◯ What to wear

You will need to dress for the theatre.

Girls wore a knee-length dress and woollen stockings. Long hair was curled into ringlets.

Boys wore knickerbockers, jacket, waistcoat, shirt and tie.

▲ *A Gaiety Girl poster*

◯ Your Destination

London's West End is full of theatres, and the Gaiety is at its heart. It is run by manager George Edwardes, a man with a big bushy moustache and, very often, a big cigar, too.

❋ *Edwardes' theatre is famous for its 'Gaiety Girls' – dancers who, when they are not performing, can be seen partying around town with wealthy young gentlemen.*

❋ *After the theatre, wealthy guests might go on to the bar of one of London's luxury hotels, such as the Savoy or the Ritz, where a fountain sometimes flows with champagne.*

❋ *West End actors and actresses have become nationwide celebrities, thanks to newspapers and printed posters. Tonight actress Gertie Millar will be starring in The Gaiety's production of The Orchid.*

▲ *Wealthy theatre-goers share a box at a production.*

Take a tram… or a car or a bicycle!

London has grown so big that it has become a county in its own right, and its streets are thronging with traffic. In 1900 it was mostly horse drawn, and there were around 300,000 working horses in the town. By 1915 this will change completely and most traffic will be motor-driven.

In 1903 there are still lots of horse-drawn trams and carriages, but also electric trams running along rails above ground. Bicycles are common on the streets, but in 1903 there are now occasional cars, too. There is no driving test or speed limit for cars yet, so pedestrians must watch out!

▲ *Most of the traffic filling this London street in 1903 is still horse-drawn.*

Back to the 21st century: Theatreland

London is still famous for its entertainment. The West End is sometimes called 'theatreland' because of its theatres, some of which date back to Edwardian times.

In the early 20th century, London became famous for its luxury hotels, restaurants and tea shops. It still is today!

Wealthy Edwardians had household servants and grand town houses. You can often see their lives recreated in movies and TV shows such as *Downton Abbey*.

▲ *Shaftesbury Avenue, shown here, is in the heart of 'Theatreland'.*

See the suburbs

Would you like a cup of tea and perhaps a slice of cake? Go on! You know you want to! After all, you are an honoured guest at the opening of Stanmore Tube Station today. The new building has been designed to look like a woodland cottage. Out here we like to think we're in the country. Lots of Londoners agree, and that's why so many are moving out of the centre of town.

LOCATION: STANMORE TUBE STATION

Cloisters Wood

Stanmore

London Road

Marsh Lane

Metro-land awaits

The Metropolitan Railway now runs from Baker Street out to the northwest of town, where there are many new estates. People call it 'Metro-land' and travel from here into town to work. It marks a big change in London life. 'Commuting' has begun!

► *The Metropolitan Railway published a series of books to encourage people to move to Metro-land.*

METRO-LAND
PRICE TWOPENCE

◯ Your Destination

For the first time in 1,000 years the population of central London is going down, as people move out to the suburbs.

✳ *For many people there is at last a chance to leave cramped rented buildings in the centre and buy their own spacious home with a garden. The houses cost between £500 and £1,000.*

✳ *Metro-land is marketed as a 'return to nature', as if people are going to live in the country villages of a bygone England. The houses are built in styles from history, such as Tudor and Georgian.*

✳ *Poems and songs are written about the wonders of Metro-land, including this song by George R. Simms: "I know a land where wild flowers grow, Near, near at hand if by train you go. Metro-land!"*

✳ *Some people are very snobbish about Metro-land, making fun of the new fake 'Tudorbethan' buildings and the way that Metro-land pretends to be countryside. But for many, it offers life in much better conditions than they have ever had in the middle of town.*

▲ **The quiet streets and large gardens of Metro-land attracted many inner-city Londoners.**

London calling

Meet Eileen. Her family have moved to a brand new Metro-land home, and for the first time she has her own bedroom. She and her family have a new radio, too. It's a big wooden-cased one, like a piece of furniture, and the whole family huddle round it to listen to broadcasts by the BBC. Eileen thinks that's truly amazing!

In 1932 the BBC begins to broadcast all over the world from its new headquarters, Broadcasting House. People in far-off lands can sit round their radios, too, listening to people talking or playing music in the heart of London.

Eileen loves to go to the new cinemas springing up around everywhere. Children go on Saturday mornings, for their own special shows.

In 1932 the BBC are experimenting with a new invention – TV. Their first show will be broadcast from London in 1936 with the words: *"Good afternoon, ladies and gentlemen. It is with great pleasure that I introduce you to the magic of television."* Performances on the first show will include an orchestra, singers and a performing horse called Pogo.

▲ **1930s radios were cased in wood or bakelite, a form of plastic.**

Back to the 21st century: Suburban sight-seeing

You can take a trip out of central London by rail or Tube to walk the streets of Metro-land or visit lots of interesting sights. Here are some of them:

- **Wembley Stadium** Tour England's national football stadium (left).

- **RAF Museum, Hendon** See over 100 aircraft on display.

- **Lawn Tennis Museum, Wimbledon** See the home of tennis and also visit nearby Wimbledon Common.

- **London Wetland Centre, Barnes** a nature reserve very near town.

- **Cutty Sark, Greenwich** Go onboard the last surviving tea clipper ship from the 1800s.

- **Syon House** A grand house with parklands in southwest London.

- **Museum of Childhood, Bethnal Green** Toys and games through the ages.

un for cov r

It is September 1940; Britain is at war and London is taking a pounding. It's dark but the street is filled with people running past you. You can hear an ear-splitting siren noise, too. It is warning that German planes have been spotted, which means that bombs will soon start to fall. You must follow the crowd to take cover in the nearest Tube Station and huddle together in the chilly gloom as best you can until the all-clear signal sounds.

LOCATION: SITE OF ALDWYCH TUBE STATION

Covent Garden

Aldwych

Strand

Somerset House

Temple Station

Wartime town

During the First World War (1914-18) London was the target of bombings by Zeppelin airships, but in the Second World War the bombings are much worse. London will suffer 57 successive nights of bombing by the German Luftwaffe (air force) during 1940, a period of the war called the Blitz.

◀ *Bombed out families rescued what they could from their wrecked homes.*

※ Don't forget to take your gas mask with you. Every man, woman and child has been issued with one, to protect against a possible gas attack. There are even special tiny gas masks for babies. In the end there will be no gas attacks on London.

◯ Your Destination

Seventy-nine Underground stations were are used as shelters during the Blitz. They are all fitted with beds, but over 100,000 people use them, so conditions are cramped. The beds are set up along the platforms.

※ You are at the Aldwych Tube Station. During the Blitz it has its own canteen, first-aid station and even a library. It's also the secret wartime store for priceless treasures from the Victoria and Albert Museum.

※ Not everyone hides in the Underground. Some families have Andersen shelters in their gardens — metal huts half-buried in the ground, with earth thrown over the top to give protection from blasts. They are big enough for six people to sit inside.

▲ *Londoners sought safety on Tube Station platforms during the Blitz.*

▲ *Fires raged out of control during the Blitz as the fire services struggled to cope.*

Danger on the streets

ARP wardens patrol the streets checking that the blackout rules are being followed. Everyone must cover their windows at night to stop light providing an easy target for bombers.

There are no street lights, and accidents often happen as cars drive without headlamps and people stumble along in the darkness.

The worst nights

The whole of London was bombed but the docklands and the East End suffered most during the Blitz. On 29th December there was a 'second fire of London' in the old City when the bombs created a firestorm. By the end of the Blitz in May 1941, 20,000 people had lost their lives in London and more than a million homes had been destroyed.

Back to the 21st century: Imperial War Museum

At the Imperial War Museum at Southwark you can find out what it was like to sit in an Andersen shelter during an air raid and discover the story of London's wartime children.

On the Imperial War Museum website (see p. 63) you can explore an interactive map to find out what happened in different areas of London during the Blitz.

▲ **Two huge naval guns are displayed outside the Imperial War Museum in London.**

Fight from home

You are in a busy room at the end of a long corridor. Phones are ringing and people are bustling about or studying large maps. There is no daylight down here because you are in an underground bunker, the Cabinet War Rooms, where British leader Winston Churchill is meeting with his War Cabinet of advisors. Together they are planning their next move to defeat Nazi Germany. You must keep your location a secret. The enemy does not know about it!

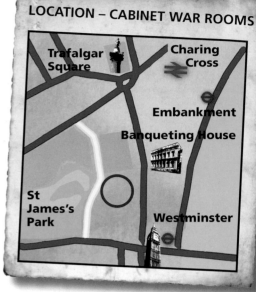

LOCATION – CABINET WAR ROOMS

Trafalgar Square
Charing Cross
Embankment
Banqueting House
St James's Park
Westminster

Life for Londoners

Out on the streets of London, life isn't easy. Food is rationed and shoppers must queue to exchange ration tokens for staples such as meat, bread and milk. Clothing is rationed, too. On the 'Home Front', as life in wartime Britain is called, everyone must 'make do and mend'.

◀ *A queue to spend ration tokens on food.*

※ *It is from the Cabinet War Rooms that Churchill speaks by secret telephone link to his vital ally US President Roosevelt. He sometimes has to sleep here, too. Hitler never guesses that his enemy's hiding place is so close to Number 10 Downing Street.*

◯ Your Destination

The Cabinet War Rooms are below ground in Whitehall but they are a closely guarded secret. Churchill and his Cabinet meet here, sometimes late at night, and Churchill presides over tense meetings.

※ *The King and Queen have also stayed in London for the whole of the war, even though Buckingham Palace has been repeatedly bombed.*

※ *Wartime London is the destination for troops and refugees from all over the world. In 1944 lots of US troops arrive, ready to invade Europe on D-Day. London's children like them because they hand out chewing gum, never tried by the locals before!*

▲ *Inside one of the Cabinet War Rooms during the Second World War.*

Meet Johnnie

Johnnie has been evacuated from his home in London. Like many children, he has been sent to the countryside for his own safety.

Johnnie travelled by train along with lots of other children, each one with a label round their neck like a parcel. When he got to his destination he was taken to a village hall and people came along to choose which child or children they would take home.

Johnnie's mum has sent him letters, and he was hopeful he could soon go home, but the Germans have started launching flying rockets on London and he will have to wait a little longer before he can return.

The V-1 and V-2 flying bombs are launched from far away and when they reach their target they cause great destruction. They are Hitler's final airborne attack on London before the war ends in 1945.

◄ *A feared V-1 flying bomb. When it ran out of fuel, it fell to the ground causing terrible destruction.*

Back to the 21st century: Visit some museums

▼ *At the Cabinet War Rooms you can see rooms lined with the maps used during the Second World War.*

You can visit Churchill's Cabinet War Rooms in Whitehall and see where the defence of Britain was planned. Everything is still there, just as it was. You can even see the chair that Churchill sat in during meetings, along with the scratch marks he made on the chair's arms, perhaps when meetings were tense.

By the end of the war over three million British people had experienced evacuation, many of them Londoners. Find out about their lives and the experiences of those left behind in the World War Two rooms at the Museum of London.

Get with it

You've arrived where it's at, baby! You're in Carnaby Street, the London home of 1960s fashion. The latest pop music is drifting out of the shops, where young celebrities such as the Rolling Stones and the Beatles buy their brightly-coloured flared trousers. London has a new worldwide reputation as a centre of fun.

LOCATION – CARNABY STREET

Oxford Circus

Great Marlborough Street

Regent Street

London gets livelier

In the 1950s London began to recover from war. By the 1960s it has got the nickname 'swinging London' because of its pop culture. It has become more multicultural, too. People have come to live there from former British colonies such as the West Indies, India and Pakistan.

◀ *West Indian Brixton or Indian Southall caption?*

○ Your Destination

Carnaby Street is lined with boutiques, the new name for small designer fashion stores. Its street sign is now world famous as a symbol of the swinging '60s.

❋ *Young fashion designer Mary Quant has her store here. She has invented the biggest fashion hits of the 1960s – the mini skirt and hot pants.*

❋ *Keep an eye out for Mick Jagger of the Rolling Stones. He sometimes shops here when he is not performing round the corner at the Marquee Club in Wardour Street.*

❋ *London hairdresser Vidal Sassoon created the geometric hairstyle that Mary Quant wore, and has helped to make hairdressing a big part of the London fashion scene.*

❋ *The Beatles are the biggest band of the time, and you'll hear their music in the boutiques and record shops. They are a Liverpool band but they will record their final album at Abbey Road in London at the end of the 1960s.*

Lord John

▶ **Carnaby Street in the 1960s. It is located close to Oxford Circus and Regent Street.**

1960s snapshots

The year 1966 is a fantastic one for the England football team, who win the World Cup at Wembley, beating Germany 4-2.

▲ *Mary Quant (above) and Twiggy (below), faces of the 1960s*

▲ *England captain, Bobby Moore, kisses the World Cup in 1966.*

Young Londoner Twiggy becomes the face of the 1960s, the world's top model.

The King's Road is another fashion hotspot in the 1960s, where you can find the very latest styles.

Heathrow Airport starts to grow in the 1960s, as air travel becomes popular. More and more tourists begin to arrive in London to see its famous sights.

Back to the 21st century: Fashion in museums

You can find out about the history of fashion at the Victoria and Albert Museum and the London Museum of Fashion. At the Design Museum you can learn about design and do some creative workshops.

▶ *An exhibition of the work of French shoe designer Christian Louboutin at the Design Museum.*

Population: 8 million approx.

Walk the riverside

You are back in the present and, if you look down, you will see the River Thames flowing beneath your feet. You are standing on the Millennium Bridge, with a view of the river snaking past some of London's greatest buildings, old and new. The people walking past you will be from all over the world. Some will live here and others will be visiting this vibrant world-class city.

LOCATION – ON MILLENNIUM BRIDGE

Blackfriars   St Paul's

Globe Theatre

Southwark

⊙ What to wear

You can wear anything you want! London is one of the world's most fashionable capitals and it has many inhabitants from all over the globe, so feel free to choose your own outfit.

In London, traditional clothes are worn alongside high fashion.

⊙ Your Destination

New pathways and building work have made London's riverside a great place to explore on foot or by boat.

✳ There are lots of riverside warehouses, now flats, with interesting names such as Tea Trade Wharf and Cinnamon Wharf. You can guess what goods were once unloaded there!

✳ Canary Wharf has been converted into a second business district in London. Once London made its money from the docks, but now its main businesses are financial.

✳ London is low-lying and the Thames is tidal. Parts of London could flood if it weren't for the Thames Barrier, ten huge steel flood gates that can be raised to keep flood waters back.

✳ When the Millennium Bridge was first opened, the motion of people walking across it made it wobble and sway! Engineers fixed the problem, but for a while it had the nickname 'the wobbly bridge'.

▶ **Canary Wharf has some of the tallest buildings in London.**

54

River reborn

The Thames in London was once a dead river, so polluted by sewage and industrial waste that nothing could live in it. But hard work to improve it has led to a dramatic restoration of the river's health.

Over a hundred species of fish live in the river, and dolphins, seals and otters have all been seen in London. Salmon have started to migrate (travel) up the river from the sea.

▲ Salmon, seals (top) and dolphins (left) have all been recorded in the River Thames since it became less polluted.

Back to the 21st century: Wetlands and docklands

At the Museum of London Docklands you can discover the history of the river and the Londoners who have worked on it and around it.

The London Wetlands Centre is a beautiful river wildlife reserve not far from the city centre, where you can roam amongst nature.

River boats can take you along the Thames in either direction, so you can see London's sites from the water.

▲ The Museum of London Docklands is housed in a warehouse, built to store sugar, coffee and rum 200 years ago.

Look across London

If you're scared of heights you might want to keep your eyes shut but if you open them you will find yourself 309.7m (1016ft) up, with a 100km (60 mile) view around London. The time machine has brought you to the top of the Shard, Britain's tallest building. The very top of the tower was completed in 2012, and a workman (in a safety harness) did a dance on one of the construction beams that day. Would you like to do a dance, or would you rather get back into the time machine as quickly as possible?

LOCATION - TOP OF THE SHARD

London Bridge Station

London changes

London never stays the same for long. New buildings appear, or old ones get redeveloped. Several new buildings have become sites that everybody recognises.

✳ 30 St Mary Axe is another famous 21st century London building. It is nicknamed 'the gherkin' because of its shape. It is 180m (590ft) high, and its design allows daylight to flood inside, to save on electricity bills. It is covered in enough glass to cover five football pitches.

◯ **Your Destination**

The Shard can be seen for miles around, as can some other tall buildings new to London's landscape.

✳ The architect who designed the Shard was partly inspired by an old painting of London that showed church spires and tall ships' masts.

✳ The crane drivers who helped build the Shard were working nearly 305m (1,000ft) up in the air every day and could feel the vibrations from jet passenger aeroplanes flying above them as they worked.

▲ Known as 'the gherkin', 30 St Mary Axe houses offices.

◀ Shown under construction here, the Shard mainly contains offices.

The icon of art

In 2000 the Tate Modern art gallery opened in an old power station on the south bank of the River Thames. It soon became one of the world's most popular art galleries, with over four million people coming to see its modern art every year.

The main hall of the gallery is called the Turbine Hall because it once housed giant electricity turbines. In 2003 around two million people came to see the Weather Project there. A giant circle of lamps shone brightly at one end to create a sun, and visitors loved to lie on the ground to see themselves in mirrors on the ceiling. They appeared as tiny moving black shadows against the light.

▶ *The mesmerising Weather Project, an art installation created by Danish artist Olafur Eliasson at Tate Modern.*

Back to the 21st century: Farms, fashion and fun

▼ *City farms, including the one at Spitalfields, give Londoners the chance to see farm animals in the city.*

Here are a few London attractions that definitely weren't around in former times.

City farms are now popular around London, giving everyone a taste of the countryside in the city. Londoners of the past would never have been very far from fields and farms.

▲ *Sand is brought to the riverbank to create the feeling of a seaside resort, just for fun.*

New shops, restaurants and markets start to appear when areas of London become fashionable to visit. Shoreditch in east London is an example of an area that was once very quiet and is now full of fashion stores, galleries and cafés.

In summer a beach sometimes appears along the south bank of the River Thames!

Peer into the future

London is a lot more crowded now than it ever was, and yet strangely it's less noisy. That's because the old diesel-powered cars and buses that used to clog the streets have gone. Talking of streets, they are more in shadow than ever before as they are lined with many giant skyscrapers. Hold on, there's a problem... Is that snow in July?

The time machine is cheating here. It can't *really* go into the future so it's going to show you some ideas about what might happen.

People power

London is likely to be a megacity in the future. A megacity has over 10 million people in it, and London will have at least that number. People will come here from all over the world and they will need places to live, perhaps in more hi-rise buildings. Tokyo is already a megacity with over 13 million people. Perhaps London will get more hi-rise buildings like Tokyo.

▶ *Megacity Tokyo's skyline is crowded with hi-rise structures.*

Quiet cars

A lot more of the centre of London is likely to be restricted to pedestrians, and the cars and buses of the future could one day

be super-quiet electric vehicles. They may well be steered by computer, and so won't need a driver.

▲ *Shape of the future – the London 2012 Olympic Park is full of pedestrianised spaces.*

Smart buildings

It could well be normal for London buildings of the future to be full of computer sensors, so they can alter their lighting and heating automatically and create their own water and air, rather like a spaceship. They might even have walls that register who you are and change colour to suit your mood or speak to you as you go past.

▲ *Futuristic interactive buildings featured in the 2002 film* Minority Report.

Danger for London

Many people think that the world's climate is altering – and that could mean big changes for London. Will it become much warmer or much colder? Will sea levels rise and threaten the city? Nobody knows for sure.

▲ Global warming could see London at high risk of flooding and with a much colder climate.

▲ Climate change might make London into a habitat fit for jungle plants.

New secrets discovered

As more and more foundations are dug for new buildings, new archaeological secrets will be revealed around the city. Perhaps we will discover treasures such as ancient buried tombs and coins, as well as settlements we never knew existed. As London grows, its distant past and its old inhabitants could reappear.

'Hello! Nice to see you again!'

Back to the 21st century: Go back in time for real!

Perhaps Londoners will discover how to really travel in time, in which case they could be back to see us any time soon!

▶ Children from the 22nd century might be able to take time-travel holidays in the future!

▲ Perhaps London will look like this artist's imagined drawing of the future.

Glossary

Abbey A large Christian church.

Albertopolis An area of London around Kensington redeveloped by the Victorians to include museums and a concert hall.

Amphitheatre A Roman stadium, where gladiators fought.

Anglo-Saxons People who arrived in England from northern Europe and settled there during the late 400s.

Apothecary A maker of herbal medicines.

Apprentice A young person learning a trade from a more experienced person.

Archaeology The study of history by excavating sites and studying objects.

Astronomical clock A clock that displays star signs as well as the time.

Bankside An area south of the Thames in Southwark, along the riverbank.

Baroque A style of building in the 1600s, with lots of stone carving and wall paintings.

Barrage balloon A large balloon used as defence from enemy aircraft.

Basilica A Roman town hall.

Black Death A plague that killed many people across Britain between 1348 and 1349.

Blitz A period during the Second World War, from September 1940 to May 1941, when British cities were bombed by the German air force.

Boudica Queen of the Iceni tribe who led a revolt against the Romans in 60CE.

Bronze Age A period from 2200–750BCE when people began to settle and farm.

Celtic The name now given to the people who lived in Britain in the period before the Romans arrived in 43CE.

City of London The part of London once inside the ancient city walls.

Coif A type of woollen cap worn by women in the 1500s.

Convent A religious community of nuns.

Coronation The crowning of a monarch.

Dissolution The closing down of monasteries and convents, ordered by Henry VIII in 1536.

Domus A Roman town house.

Edwardian A period of time in the early 20th century, when Edward VII reigned.

Evacuation Sending people away from an area to avoid danger. Many children were evacuated from London during the Second World War.

Forum The main open meeting square in a Roman city.

Gothic A style of building popular in Victorian times. Gothic buildings look rather like medieval cathedrals.

Great Exhibition A big festival held in London in 1851, showcasing art and science.

Great Slaughter A Danish Viking attack on London in 842CE.

Groundling Audience-members who stood in front of the stage to watch a Tudor play.

Guild Groups of skilled craftsmen who organised themselves together in medieval times.

Hanoverians A family who ruled Britain between 1714 and 1837.

Home Front The name given to life in Britain during the Second World War.

Iceni A Celtic tribe from East Anglia, who fought the Romans.

Iron Age A period from 750BCE to 42CE when people began to make iron tools.

Keep A square building in the middle of a castle.

Knights Templar A powerful group of fighting monks with a London headquarters.

Legionary A Roman soldier.

Livery Companies The modern name for the old medieval Guilds, groups of skilled workers.

Londinium The Roman name for London.

Longships Boats that carried Viking warriors from Scandinavia to Britain.

Loom A hand-operated machine for weaving cloth.

Lord Mayor The mayor of the City of London (not the mayor of the whole of London).

Lundenburgh A name used for London in the 800s.

Lundenwic The Anglo-Saxon name for London in about 700CE.

Medieval The period of European history between 1066 and 1485.

Meridian The imaginary line that separates the eastern and western halves (hemispheres) of the world.

Metro-land The name given to new housing built to the northwest of London in the 1920s and 30s.

Mint A place where coins are manufactured.

Mithras A Roman god popular with Roman soldiers.

Monastery A religious community of monks.

Mosaic A picture made from tiny coloured squares.

Normans French-speaking nobles who conquered England in 1066.

Observatory A building used for housing a telescope, to study the stars.

Offering A present given in honour of a god or goddess.

Olympics A four-yearly international sporting event, held in London in 2012.

Ordinances of Eltham A set of rules governing daily life at Hampton Court.

Palace of Westminster The medieval palace of the English kings, now rebuilt as the Houses of Parliament.

Palladian A type of building style used in the 1700s, with Roman-style pillars, sash windows and streets shaped in circles or crescents.

Pit A building used to stage fights between dogs and either bears or bulls.

Plague A fatal disease that killed many people in London and other parts of the country from medieval times onwards.

Plague pit A large pit where the bodies of plague victims were buried together.

Plantagenets A family of English rulers that came to the throne in 1216.

Pottage A mushy vegetable and meat stew eaten by many ordinary people in medieval times.

Props Objects used on the stage during a play.

Protestants People who follow the Protestant religion.

Puritans People who followed a strict form of the Protestant religion in the 1600s.

Quay The side of a river or sea port, where goods are unloaded and loaded on boats.

Rationing Restricting everyday items such as food and clothing when they are in short supply. Britain had rationing during the Second World War.

Real tennis An early type of tennis played in the 1500s.

Romanesque A type of building style used by the Normans.

Roman Catholics People who follow the Catholic religion, led by the Pope based in Rome.

Scaffold The wooden structure set up for public executions.

Steam train A train that is powered by steam created when water is heated up by coal being burnt onboard the train.

Stolla A Roman tunic worn by women.

Stuarts A family who ruled Britain from 1603 to 1714.

Tavern A public house, where you could drink alcohol.

Theatreland A name sometimes given to London's West End, where there are lots of theatres.

Thief-taker An informer who got a reward for turning in criminals in the early 1700s, before there was a police force.

Thornhill A marshy island where Westminster Abbey was built.

Traitors' Gate A gate leading from the River Thames into the Tower of London.

Tram A bus that runs on rails or overhead lines.

Transportation The sending of prisoners to penal colonies (working prison communities) in America, Australia and Africa.

Tribe A group of people who live together under a leader.

Tudors A family who ruled England and Wales between 1485 and 1603.

Walbrook A stream that runs into the Thames, now mainly flowing under the streets of London in the City area.

Victoria Queen of Britain between 1837 and 1901.

Viking Warriors and settlers from Scandinavia.

V-bomb A type of German flying bomb aimed at London in 1944.

Warehouse A building where goods are stored.

Watling Street A Roman road leading north from London.

Time traveller's timeline

2200–750BCE Bronze Age. People begin to settle and farm around the River Thames.

750BCE–43CE Iron Age. Tribes lived in different territories around the River Thames.

43 The Romans arrive and create a settlement called Londinium (London).

60–61 Boudica leads the Iceni and other tribes in an attack on Londinium.

100 Londinium flourishes once again, as a port.

410 Roman rule ends.

Late 400s Saxons arrive from northern Europe and begin to settle around the River Thames.

604 Christianity takes hold, and London gets its first Bishop.

700 Anglo-Saxon Lundenwic is in the area now called Covent Garden.

842 Danish Vikings attack, in an event called the 'Great Slaughter'.

878 Anglo-Saxon King Alfred defeats the Vikings and fortifies the city. It is called Lundenburgh.

1014 Anglo-Saxon King Aethelred defeats the Vikings by pulling down London Bridge.

1066 The Normans invade and William the Conquerer takes the throne.

1078 The Tower of London is begun.

1216 King John gives the City of London a charter, an important list of rights.

1348–1349 The Black Death plague hits the country and many die.

1381 The Peasants' Revolt. Rebels march on London.

1485 The Tudor dynasty begins after the Wars of the Roses.

1517 The beginnings of the Protestant Reformation in Europe, when some countries turned away from Roman Catholicism.

1536 King Henry VIII orders the destruction of the Catholic monasteries across his kingdom, including London.

1603 Elizabeth I dies, ending the reign of the Tudors and beginning the reign of the Stuarts.

1642 London takes the side of Parliament during the English Civil War.

1649 Charles I is executed in London.

1663 The Great Plague hits London.

1666 The Great Fire of London.

1697 A rebuilt St Paul's Cathedral opens.

1750 Bow Street Runners are formed, the first official police in London.

1787 For the first time, people convicted of a crime are sent from London to penal colonies in Australia.

1836 The first London railway.

1838 Queen Victoria is crowned.

1845 Many immigrants arrive from Ireland to escape the Great Famine there.

1851 The Great Exhibition, a giant show held at Crystal Palace.

1858 The year of the 'Great Stink'. The smell in London is so bad, that Joseph Bazalgette is asked to rebuild the sewer system.

1863 The first London underground line opens.

1868 Public hanging ends.

1889 London is so big it is recognised as a separate county, with its own elected local government.

1914–18 The First World War.

1939–45 The Second World War. London suffers bombing.

1948 The Olympics are held in London.

1952 London suffers terrible pollution, called the Great Smog.

1984 The Thames Barrier is opened, to prevent flooding in London.

1999 The Dome, the London Eye and the Millennium Bridge open to celebrate the Millennium.

2012 The Olympics are held in London.

Websites

http://www.museumoflondon.org.uk/learning/features_facts/digging/
See a reconstruction of Roman Londinium and play the Londinium game.

http://www.museumoflondonprints.com
See photos of the museum's collection, spanning London's history.

http://www.archaeology.co.uk/the-timeline-of-britain/the-story-of-roman-london.htm
See some photos of Roman digs in London.

http://lordmayorshow.org/history/gog-and-magog
Read more about the legendary London giants.

http://www.hrp.org.uk/
Find out about historic royal palaces, including the Tower of London, Hampton Court, the Banqueting House, Kensington Palace and Kew Palace. Information on Hampton Court includes some Tudor recipes to download and try out.

http://www.bog-standard.org/pupils_history.aspx
Find out how the British went to the lavatory through history.

http://www.parliament.uk/visiting/online-tours/virtualtours
Take an interactive tour of the Palace of Westminster, including Westminster Hall and Big Ben.

http://www.royalcollection.org.uk/visit/buckinghampalace
Find out what it's like inside Buckingham Palace.

http://www.londontourist.org/historic.html
A useful list of historic London buildings you can visit, with links.

http://www.nhm.ac.uk/kids-only/index.html
The Natural History Museum website has a kid's section, with games and quizzes.

http://www.eyewitnesstohistory.com/pflondonfire.htm
Read Samuel Pepys' account of the Great Fire of London in 1666.

http://www.themonument.info
Find out about the Great Fire of London and see a timelapse panorama of the City of London.

http://www.bl.uk/learning/histcitizen/georgians/georgianhome.html
A very good reference site for life in Georgian London.

http://www.stand-and-deliver.org.uk
Find out about London's most famous highwaymen.

http://www.bl.uk/londoninmaps
A virtual exhibition of London maps through the ages, from the British Library.

http://www.geffrye-museum.org.uk/period-rooms-and-gardens/explore-rooms/
See London rooms through the centuries, from 1600 to today.

http://www.ltmuseum.co.uk
The website of the London Transport Museum. Online there are paper models to download and build, and games to play.

http://www.youtube.com/watch?v=v-5Ts_i164c
See a film of a London street scene in 1903.

http://1940.iwm.org.uk/?page_id=18
An Imperial War Museum map showing places destroyed around London during the Blitz.

http://kids.tate.org.uk/
Join in all kinds of fun art activities online, linked to the Tate Modern.

http://www.timeout.com/london/feature/904/london-by-area
Find out what's going on in different areas of London.

http://www.timeout.com/london/kids/
Ideas for kids and families when visiting London.

Index